INKSPIRE

TRAVELS

Savvy Tips, Regional Eats, and Scenic Escapes from Italy's Medieval Gem

BOLOGNA
Travel Guide
2025

INKSPIRE

Copyright

Disclaimer

The author and publisher have made every effort to ensure the accuracy and completeness of the information contained in this book. However, they assume no responsibility for errors, inaccuracies, omissions, or any other inconsistencies herein. This book is not intended to provide legal, financial, or other professional advice.

About Our Authors

Jeremy Johnson is an acclaimed author in the world of travel writing, celebrated for his vivid and immersive narratives. With a deep curiosity and a gift for storytelling, he brings destinations to life by capturing their true essence and hidden soul. Far more than just a source of tips, his guidebooks inspire mindful exploration and a genuine respect for cultural richness. Whether you're a globe-trotting adventurer or a weekend wanderer, Jeremy's work invites you to travel deeper and connect more meaningfully with the world around you.

Gary Saint is an award-winning travel writer and photographer whose journeys have spanned over 60 countries across six continents during his rich, decade-long career. Known for his vivid storytelling and adventurous spirit, Gary crafts narratives that go far beyond typical travel advice. His work artfully combines useful insights with captivating experiences, all while highlighting his deep admiration for the world's cultures and landscapes. A strong believer in travel as a force for good, Gary's guides encourage readers—from seasoned globetrotters to curious newcomers—to explore with purpose and embrace the wonders of our planet.

BOLOGNA

SCAN THE QR CODE

- Open your phone's camera app
- Most smartphones have a built-in QR scanner in the camera.
- Point the camera at the QR code
- Make sure the code is clear and within the frame.
- Wait for the notification
- A link or message should pop up on your screen.
- Tap the notification
- This will open the link or content in your browser or a relevant app.
- Follow the instructions on the screen
- You will be taken to a Google Maps, app where you can now click on your current location to get to your destination.

Table of Content

Introduction

The moment I stepped off the train at Bologna Centrale, a wave of anticipation washed over me. The crisp spring air carried a mix of scents—freshly baked bread, roasted coffee beans, and something unmistakably ancient, like history itself lingering in the breeze. I pulled my jacket tighter as I navigated through the bustling station, the hum of Italian chatter blending seamlessly with the rhythmic clatter of footsteps on cobblestones outside. This was my first real encounter with Bologna, a city I had long heard described as Italy's "culinary capital" and a place where centuries-old traditions still pulse vibrantly in everyday life.

But nothing had prepared me for what awaited just beyond the station doors.

As I emerged into Piazza Maggiore, the city's grand central square, my eyes were instantly drawn upward to the towering medieval structures framing the space. The imposing silhouette of the Basilica di San Petronio loomed ahead, its unfinished facade telling stories of ambition and resilience. Nearby, the iconic Two Towers—Asinelli and Garisenda—reached skyward, leaning ever so slightly as if whispering secrets from the past. The porticoes stretched endlessly on either side, inviting exploration beneath their shaded embrace.

I remember the moment I first traced my fingers along the warm terracotta bricks of the portico—so familiar yet full of mystery—and felt the pulse of the city beneath my skin. Bologna is a place where every corner holds a story, where the past and present intertwine in unexpected ways. The energy here is unlike anywhere else I've been. It's lively yet intimate, historic but refreshingly unpretentious.

That first evening, wandering the labyrinth of narrow streets, I stumbled upon a tiny osteria tucked away from the tourist throngs. The aroma of rich ragù simmering for hours pulled me inside, and I found myself savoring plates of homemade tagliatelle as the chatter of locals filled the air. It was in that moment, over food that tasted like a warm embrace, that I realized Bologna isn't just a destination—it's an experience. A city that seeps into your senses and invites you to become part of its story.

Welcome to Bologna

There's a certain magic to Bologna that draws you in the moment you begin to unravel its layers. Nestled in the heart of Italy's Emilia-Romagna region, Bologna is often overshadowed by the country's more famous cities like Rome, Florence, and Venice. Yet, this vibrant city, with its striking medieval architecture, rich culinary heritage, and warm, welcoming spirit, offers an experience all its own—one that has quietly captured the hearts of travelers and locals alike.

Walking through Bologna, it's easy to see why it's often called "La Dotta, La Rossa, La Grassa"—the Learned, the Red, the Fat. These nicknames hint at the city's university heritage, its signature terracotta rooftops, and its reputation as a food lover's paradise. But Bologna is far more than these labels. It's a city that embraces contrasts: centuries-old traditions sit side by side with lively student culture, elegant palaces share space with cozy street cafes, and bustling markets hum alongside quiet, shady porticoes.

If you're reading this in 2025, you're about to embark on a journey to a city that has been quietly reinventing itself while holding fast to its roots.

Bologna today is a dynamic blend of history, innovation, and culture—a place where you can feast on some of Italy's most authentic cuisine, explore cobblestone streets that have witnessed centuries of change, and connect with a community proud of its past and excited for the future.

Why Bologna in 2025?

2025 is an exciting time to visit Bologna, for several compelling reasons. First, the city is in the midst of a cultural and culinary renaissance. Recent efforts have breathed new life into neighborhoods, markets, and public spaces, making Bologna more accessible, vibrant, and visitor-friendly than ever before. The city's commitment to sustainable tourism and urban innovation means that travelers can enjoy their visit while supporting local businesses and minimizing environmental impact.

One standout aspect of Bologna in 2025 is its growing reputation as a hub for slow travel and authentic experiences. Tourists are no longer content with just ticking off famous landmarks; they want to immerse themselves fully, tasting, learning, and participating in the local way of life. Bologna answers that call perfectly. From artisanal food producers crafting traditional balsamic vinegar and Parmigiano Reggiano cheese nearby, to centuries-old universities fostering fresh ideas, the city offers an unparalleled depth of experience.

Additionally, Bologna's strategic location makes it an ideal base for exploring the wider Emilia-Romagna region and beyond. High-speed trains connect you to Florence, Milan, Venice, and Rome within a few hours, while nearby countryside offers rolling hills, vineyards, and historic towns waiting to be discovered. In 2025, travel infrastructure is smoother than ever, with improved transit options and enhanced traveler services.

Bologna's calendar in 2025 is packed with festivals, art exhibitions, and culinary events that highlight the city's vibrant creative scene. Whether it's jazz performances, film screenings, or food fairs, there's always something happening that brings locals and visitors together in celebration of Bologna's rich culture. This dynamic atmosphere gives the city a youthful energy, making it appealing for all kinds of travelers—from solo adventurers to families and couples.

Finally, Bologna stands out for its genuine warmth and hospitality. Despite being a major Italian city, it has avoided the impersonal feel that can sometimes accompany mass tourism. Here, you are not just a visitor; you're a guest invited to share in traditions passed down through generations. Locals are proud of their city and eager to share its stories, whether over a plate of tortellini in a centuries-old trattoria or a stroll under the city's iconic porticoes.

Top Reasons to Visit Bologna

What makes Bologna so special? What draws people here year after year? While everyone's travel priorities are different, several core reasons make Bologna a must-see destination in 2025.

1. The Food

Bologna is synonymous with Italian cuisine, and rightly so. It's the birthplace of ragù alla bolognese (the meat sauce known worldwide as "Bolognese"), as well as handmade pasta like tortellini and tagliatelle. Food here is a celebration of local ingredients and time-honored recipes. But Bologna's culinary scene is not stuck in the past—it's also a playground for innovative chefs blending tradition with modern flair. From elegant dining rooms to casual street food stalls, every meal is an opportunity to savor authentic flavors.

2. Rich History and Architecture

Few cities wear their history as proudly as Bologna. Walking through its streets, you encounter Roman ruins, medieval towers, Renaissance palaces, and Baroque churches. The Two Towers stand as silent sentinels over the city, while the labyrinthine porticoes—stretching for nearly 40 kilometers—offer a distinctive architectural feature unique to Bologna. These covered walkways have sheltered residents and visitors alike for centuries, creating a cityscape unlike any other.

3. Vibrant Cultural Scene

Bologna is a city of artists, musicians, writers, and thinkers. Its university, one of the oldest in Europe, has attracted scholars for nearly a thousand years. This intellectual energy permeates the city, inspiring theaters, galleries, and festivals. The MAMbo Museum of Modern Art and the Bologna Jazz Festival are just two examples of the thriving cultural offerings that make Bologna alive and ever-changing.

4. Walkability and Charm

Unlike many large cities, Bologna is eminently walkable. Its compact historic center invites exploration on foot, with surprises tucked around every corner—whether a tucked-away piazza, a vibrant market stall, or a quaint café. The pedestrian-friendly streets make it easy to soak in the atmosphere and discover hidden gems at your own pace.

5. Proximity to Other Destinations

Bologna's location offers easy access to other iconic Italian cities and lesser-known treasures. In less than an hour, you can be in Modena sampling world-famous balsamic vinegar, Parma with its culinary delights, or Ferrara's Renaissance splendor. The nearby Apennine Mountains beckon nature lovers with hiking trails and stunning views.

6. Local Traditions and Festivals

Throughout the year, Bologna comes alive with festivals that celebrate food, art, music, and local customs. Participating in these events offers a glimpse into the soul of the city and connects visitors with its vibrant community. From the Festa di San Petronio honoring the city's patron saint to the contemporary Bologna Design Week, there's always something to experience.

7. Warm Hospitality

Above all, what makes Bologna memorable is its people. The Bolognesi are proud, friendly, and approachable, eager to share their city's treasures with visitors. Their warmth transforms a simple trip into a lasting connection.

How to Use This Guide

This book is crafted to be your companion before and during your journey to Bologna. It's organized to provide you with everything you need to know—from practical tips to hidden gems—so you can tailor your experience to your interests and style of travel.

You'll find detailed neighborhood guides to help you navigate the city's unique districts, insider recommendations on where to eat, shop, and explore, and advice on cultural etiquette to make your interactions smooth and enjoyable. I've also included comprehensive sections on transportation, day trips, and local events, ensuring you can maximize your time without missing out on must-see attractions.

Each chapter is designed to flow logically, whether you're planning ahead or reading on the go. If you're a foodie, dive right into the culinary chapter; history buffs will appreciate the deep dive into architecture and landmarks; and those interested in local life will find festivals and cultural experiences particularly rewarding.

Practical advice, such as the best times to visit, transportation options, and safety tips, are woven throughout the guide, offering both newcomers and seasoned travelers peace of mind.

Planning Your Perfect Trip to Bologna

Planning a trip to Bologna is as exciting as the journey itself. This city, with its rich tapestry of history, culture, and culinary delights, welcomes travelers throughout the year. Yet, knowing when to visit, how to get there, and what to prepare can transform your trip from ordinary to extraordinary. In this section, I'll walk you through the essential steps for planning your perfect visit, sharing insights on the best seasons, transportation options, practical travel details, and packing tips that will have you stepping into Bologna confidently and ready to savor every moment.

Best Times to Visit: Seasonal Highlights & Festivals

Choosing the right time to visit Bologna can greatly enhance your experience. Each season paints the city in a different light, bringing unique flavors, festivals, and atmospheres.

Spring is one of Bologna's most enchanting seasons. As the chill of winter melts away, the city awakens with blooming flowers and milder temperatures, perfect for wandering its historic streets without the summer crowds. Late April through June offers pleasant weather for outdoor dining under the porticoes and exploring the markets bursting with fresh produce. Spring is also festival season here—events like the Bologna Children's Book Fair and the Festa della Repubblica on June 2nd bring vibrant energy to the city. This is an ideal time for travelers who enjoy cultural activities paired with comfortable weather.

Summer in Bologna can be warm, sometimes quite hot, but it's also a time of lively outdoor events. The city's piazzas fill with people enjoying open-air concerts, cinema nights, and street festivals. The annual Bologna Jazz Festival, usually held in late spring and early summer, showcases world-class musicians in stunning historic settings. If you don't mind the heat, summer evenings in Bologna are magical, with locals and visitors alike gathering for long dinners and passeggiata—the traditional evening stroll.

Autumn is arguably the most delicious season in Bologna. As the harvest arrives, the city's culinary scene shines brightest. Food lovers flock here for truffle fairs, wine tastings, and festivals celebrating local specialties like pumpkin and cured meats. The FICO Eataly World food park becomes a hub of activity, offering a deep dive into the flavors of Emilia-Romagna. The cooler weather and changing colors also make this a perfect time for sightseeing without the heavy tourist crowds. Autumn's golden light bathes the city's medieval towers and ancient walls in a warm glow, enhancing every photo opportunity.

Winter in Bologna is quieter, cozier, and full of festive charm. The city's Christmas markets bring a sparkle to the streets, and traditional holiday dishes feature prominently in local trattorias. While it's the coolest season, temperatures rarely dip below freezing, making it manageable for exploring. Winter visitors can also enjoy museums and galleries at a more relaxed pace, and if you're lucky, you might witness the city dusted in a rare, light snowfall—an enchanting sight against Bologna's red rooftops.

Throughout the year, Bologna's calendar offers special events that are worth timing your visit around. The Arte Fiera in January attracts art enthusiasts, while the International Film Festival in October draws cinephiles from across the globe. Checking local event listings before you book can help you align your trip with something extraordinary happening in the city.

How to Get There: Airports, Trains, and Driving Routes

Bologna's accessibility is one of its greatest assets, making it easy to reach whether you're coming from within Italy or abroad.

The main gateway is Bologna Guglielmo Marconi Airport, located just a few kilometers northwest of the city center. This airport is well-connected to major European cities and offers direct flights from many international hubs. Upon arrival, you can reach the city center quickly by taxi, airport shuttle bus, or train. The airport train station connects directly to Bologna Centrale, the city's main railway station, which is conveniently situated just a short walk or taxi ride from the heart of town.

For travelers already in Italy or Europe, train travel is often the most efficient and scenic option. Bologna Centrale is a major rail hub on Italy's high-speed train network, with frequent connections to cities such as Milan, Florence, Rome, and Venice. These trains whisk you into Bologna in under an hour from Florence or just over an hour from Milan, making day trips or multi-city tours easy to plan. The station itself is modern and well-equipped, with luggage storage, cafes, and ticket offices.

Driving to Bologna offers a different kind of freedom, especially if you plan to explore the wider Emilia-Romagna region or the nearby countryside. The city sits at the crossroads of important motorways like the A1 and A14, which link it to northern and southern Italy. However, be mindful that Bologna's historic center is a Limited Traffic Zone (Zona a Traffico Limitato, or ZTL), restricting vehicle access to residents and authorized vehicles during certain hours. It's best to park outside this zone and explore the center on foot or via public transportation. Rental car companies are plentiful at the airport and throughout the city, and roads are generally well-maintained.

For those who prefer a more adventurous route, cycling can be a rewarding way to arrive or explore the outskirts. Bologna is steadily becoming more bike-friendly, with dedicated lanes and rental options. This mode of travel offers a more intimate connection with the landscape and neighboring towns.

Visa, Currency, and Local Etiquette Essentials

Before you pack your bags, it's important to understand the practicalities of international travel to Italy and Bologna.

Most travelers from the EU, the US, Canada, Australia, and many other countries can enter Italy without a visa for stays up to 90 days. However, visa requirements vary depending on your nationality and the purpose of your visit. It's advisable to check the latest entry rules with the Italian consulate or embassy in your home country, especially as policies can change. For longer stays or different travel purposes, applying for a visa well in advance is essential.

The local currency is the Euro (€), and while credit and debit cards are widely accepted, cash is still king in many smaller shops, markets, and some restaurants. ATMs are plentiful throughout Bologna, and currency exchange offices are available, but it's wise to have some Euros on hand upon arrival for immediate expenses like taxis or tips.

Local etiquette in Bologna reflects the city's blend of tradition and warmth. Greeting with a polite "Buongiorno" (good morning) or "Buonasera" (good evening) when entering shops, restaurants, or markets is appreciated. Italians tend to dress smartly, especially in the city center and dining establishments, so while casual attire is fine during the day, a neat, stylish outfit is recommended for evenings.

When dining, it's customary to wait for everyone to be served before starting your meal and to keep conversation lively but respectful. Tipping is appreciated but not obligatory—usually a few Euros or rounding up the bill is sufficient. Being punctual is less rigid than in some cultures, but it's courteous to arrive on time for reservations and appointments.

Learning a few basic Italian phrases can go a long way in creating rapport with locals. Simple words like "grazie" (thank you), "per favore" (please), and "scusi" (excuse me) open doors to friendly interactions and richer experiences.

Packing Tips for Every Season

Packing for Bologna means balancing practicality with style. The city's charm invites leisurely strolls and dining experiences where you'll want to feel comfortable yet polished.

If you're visiting in spring, layers are your best friend. Mornings and evenings can be cool, while afternoons may warm up significantly. A light jacket, comfortable walking shoes, and a mix of short- and long-sleeve shirts will keep you prepared for changing temperatures.

Summer calls for breathable fabrics, sunglasses, and sun protection. Lightweight dresses, linen shirts, and comfortable sandals or sneakers are ideal. Remember that many churches and religious sites require modest attire, so bring a scarf or shawl to cover shoulders when visiting these places.

Autumn is versatile but leaning toward cooler weather, so packing a warm sweater, a rain jacket, and sturdy shoes is smart. The region can experience occasional showers, so having an umbrella or waterproof layers ensures you won't miss out on any adventure.

Winter in Bologna tends to be mild but damp. A warm coat, scarves, gloves, and waterproof boots will keep you comfortable. Indoor heating is common, so layering helps you adjust easily between chilly streets and cozy interiors.

No matter the season, comfortable walking shoes are essential. Bologna's cobblestone streets and expansive porticoes mean you'll be on your feet often. A daypack or crossbody bag for essentials, a reusable water bottle, and a camera or smartphone to capture moments will round out your packing list..

Neighborhoods and Districts Explored

When you arrive in Bologna, one of the first things you'll notice is that the city feels alive in every corner. The distinct neighborhoods each tell a story, offering their own unique character and experiences. Whether you're drawn to the historic grandeur of the Centro Storico, intrigued by the quieter charm of Santo Stefano, energized by the youthful buzz in the University District, or curious about the emerging scenes in Bolognina and beyond, getting to know these areas will deepen your connection to Bologna. In this section, I want to guide you through the city's neighborhoods, highlighting what makes each one special, sharing practical safety tips, and pointing out how accessible Bologna is for all travelers.

Centro Storico: The Heart of Bologna

The Centro Storico, or historic center, is the beating heart of Bologna. Stepping into this district feels like walking into a living museum, where medieval towers rise above terracotta rooftops, and ancient porticoes create cool shaded walkways for leisurely exploration. This is the area where Bologna's rich history is most palpable, and its cultural treasures are concentrated.

Wandering the narrow cobblestone streets of the Centro Storico, you'll discover architectural gems at every turn. The iconic Two Towers, Asinelli and Garisenda, stand tall here—symbols of the city's medieval past and perfect vantage points if you're up for climbing their steep staircases. Piazza Maggiore, the central square, pulses with life day and night, surrounded by historic buildings like the

Basilica di San Petronio and the Palazzo del Podestà.

Beyond the landmarks, the Centro Storico is packed with lively cafés, artisan shops, and vibrant markets. The Quadrilatero district, with its maze of narrow alleys, offers food lovers a treasure trove of fresh pasta, cured meats, cheeses, and traditional Bolognese specialties. Don't miss the chance to visit the Mercato di Mezzo for an immersive taste experience or the daily street markets for unique finds.

Despite its popularity with tourists, the Centro Storico retains an authentic atmosphere, thanks to its locals who blend everyday life with the constant hum of visitors. It's a place where you can easily spend hours just sitting at a café terrace, sipping espresso, and watching the world go by. Its walkability, dense concentration of attractions, and rich history make the historic center the ideal base for your Bologna adventure.

Santo Stefano & Saragozza: Historic and Residential Gems

Just southwest of the Centro Storico lie the charming districts of Santo Stefano and Saragozza. These neighborhoods offer a quieter, more residential feel without sacrificing cultural richness. Here, the pace slows down, inviting visitors to enjoy Bologna's relaxed side amid beautiful churches, leafy streets, and local markets.

Santo Stefano is famous for the complex of seven churches known as the Sette Chiese, a fascinating site that spans centuries of religious architecture and history. The serenity of this area contrasts with the bustling center, giving you space to reflect and admire ancient artistry in peace. The nearby Piazza Santo Stefano is a favorite spot for locals to gather, and its surrounding cafés serve up delicious treats in a laid-back setting.

Saragozza, meanwhile, is a blend of old and new. Residential streets here are lined with elegant villas and quaint shops. It's a favorite among Bologna's families and artists alike. One highlight is the Sanctuary of the Madonna di San Luca, perched atop a hill reachable via the longest portico in the world—a covered walkway stretching nearly four kilometers from the city to the sanctuary. Walking or biking up this route is a memorable experience, offering stunning views and a peaceful retreat from the urban core.

Both Santo Stefano and Saragozza provide a refreshing contrast to the city's tourist hotspots. Exploring these districts feels like peeling back another layer of Bologna's rich tapestry, where history, faith, and daily life intermingle beautifully.

University District: Student Life & Vibrant Night Scenes

No guide to Bologna would be complete without highlighting the University District. The University of Bologna is the oldest university in the Western world, dating back to 1088, and its presence still defines much of the city's energy and vibe.

This area buzzes with youthful spirit. Streets are filled with students from all over the world, creating a multicultural atmosphere that permeates cafés, bookstores, and music venues. It's here that Bologna's reputation as a hub of intellectual curiosity and artistic expression thrives.

By day, the district invites exploration of historic academic buildings like the Archiginnasio, the university's ancient seat, adorned with frescoes and the famous anatomical theatre. Bookshops and small galleries pepper the streets, showcasing Bologna's creative side.

As night falls, the University District transforms into one of the city's liveliest nightlife hubs. Bars and clubs open their doors, from casual student hangouts to jazz lounges and cocktail bars. You'll find an eclectic mix of music, from live performances to DJ sets, attracting a diverse crowd ready to enjoy the evening. Whether you want to mingle with locals, experience student culture, or simply soak in the vibrant atmosphere, this district delivers.

The University District is also a hotspot for affordable dining options. Trattorias and pizzerias offer hearty meals perfect for fueling a night out or recovering from one. This neighborhood's energy is infectious and offers a fresh, dynamic contrast to the more historic and reserved parts of Bologna.

Bolognina and Beyond: Up-and-Coming Areas to Discover

While Bologna's historic and university districts are beloved, the city's edges hold surprises that are increasingly attracting adventurous travelers. Bolognina, located north of the train station, is one of these up-and-coming neighborhoods, offering a glimpse of Bologna's evolving face.

Once considered an industrial and working-class area, Bolognina has undergone significant regeneration. Now, it buzzes with creativity, multicultural influences, and youthful energy. Street art colors many walls here, and small galleries, independent shops, and innovative eateries add fresh layers to the neighborhood's identity.

The food scene in Bolognina is particularly exciting, with a mix of traditional Italian trattorias and international cuisine from Africa, Asia, and South America, reflecting the diverse communities that call this district home. Local markets and artisan workshops foster a sense of community that visitors can tap into.

Beyond Bolognina, neighborhoods such as San Donato and Navile are also worth exploring. These areas provide authentic glimpses of everyday life away from tourist crowds, with parks, local theaters, and small venues showcasing emerging artists and musicians.

For travelers seeking to experience Bologna like a local and witness its ongoing transformation, venturing into these neighborhoods offers a rewarding perspective. It's where you'll find a more relaxed vibe, new cultural expressions, and a spirit of reinvention that complements the city's historic core.

Safety Tips and Accessibility

Bologna is generally considered a safe city for visitors, with a warm and welcoming atmosphere. However, as with any popular travel destination, staying aware and taking basic precautions ensures your experience remains enjoyable and trouble-free.

Pickpocketing can occur, especially in crowded places like markets, train stations, and tourist-heavy areas. Keeping your valuables secure, using a money belt or a bag with zippers, and staying attentive in busy spots are simple but effective measures.

Walking around at night is usually safe in well-populated districts, especially the Centro Storico and University District. However, it's best to avoid poorly lit or isolated areas after dark, particularly in less central neighborhoods.

Bologna's police presence is visible and responsive, with officers often patrolling popular districts and transportation hubs. If you ever feel uneasy or need assistance, don't hesitate to approach them—they are accustomed to helping tourists.

Regarding accessibility, Bologna is progressively improving. The city center's porticoes, while beautiful, present some challenges for those with mobility issues due to cobblestones and occasional steps. However, many museums, public buildings, and transport options are wheelchair accessible. Buses have been upgraded to accommodate passengers with disabilities, and taxi services offer accessible vehicles upon request.

For travelers with specific needs, planning ahead helps. Contacting hotels to inquire about accessibility, using apps that map accessible routes, and allowing extra time for navigating the older parts of the city can make your visit smoother.

Iconic Landmarks and Must-See Attractions

Bologna's charm is deeply rooted in its rich history, stunning architecture, and vibrant cultural scene. As you explore the city, certain landmarks naturally draw your attention—not only because of their beauty but also due to their importance in shaping the identity of this remarkable place. From the bustling heart of Piazza Maggiore to the towering medieval giants and the winding porticoes that shelter the city, each attraction tells a story waiting to be uncovered. In this section, I'll take you through Bologna's iconic landmarks and must-see sites that are essential to any visit.

Piazza Maggiore and Neptune Fountain

Piazza Maggiore is undeniably the soul of Bologna. Standing in the middle of this grand square, you immediately feel the pulse of the city's life, where history and modern-day energy collide. It's the perfect spot to start your journey through Bologna, as it brings together centuries of architectural brilliance and daily social rhythms.

Surrounded by imposing buildings such as the Palazzo d'Accursio, the Palazzo dei Notai, and the Palazzo del Podestà, Piazza Maggiore invites you to slow down and absorb its atmosphere. Locals and tourists alike gather here to enjoy everything from open-air concerts to lively markets. When the sun sets, the square's soft lighting casts a warm glow on the façades, making it an enchanting place to linger.

Dominating the piazza is the magnificent Fountain of Neptune, a Renaissance masterpiece completed in 1566. The statue of Neptune, with his trident raised, stands as a symbol of Bologna's power and maritime ambitions of the past, even though the city itself lies inland. The fountain is not just a popular photo spot but also a meeting point and a symbol of civic pride.

Taking a seat at one of the cafés lining the square, you can savor a cup of rich Italian espresso while watching the world go by, feeling connected to centuries of Bolognese life. Piazza Maggiore truly encapsulates the blend of history, culture, and vibrant social life that defines Bologna.

Piazza Maggiore

4.7 ★★★★★ 84,380 reviews
View larger map

SCAN THE QR CODE

- Open your phone's camera app
- Most smartphones have a built-in QR scanner in the camera.
- Point the camera at the QR code
- Make sure the code is clear and within the frame.
- Wait for the notification
- A link or message should pop up on your screen.
- Tap the notification
- This will open the link or content in your browser or a relevant app.
- Follow the instructions on the screen
- You will be taken to a Google Maps, app where you can now click on your current location to get to your destination.

The Two Towers (Asinelli and Garisenda)

No visit to Bologna would be complete without marveling at the city's iconic Two Towers: Asinelli and Garisenda. These towering medieval structures rise dramatically from the rooftops, providing a striking silhouette against the skyline. They stand as symbols of Bologna's medieval prosperity and the fierce competition between noble families who once built dozens of such towers as status symbols.

The taller tower, Asinelli, reaches about 97 meters and is open to visitors willing to climb its narrow, winding staircase. The ascent is not for the faint of heart—over 400 steps lead to a panoramic view that rewards every effort with sweeping vistas of the red rooftops and the surrounding Emilia-Romagna countryside. From the top, you can truly appreciate Bologna's unique urban landscape, punctuated by church domes and the distant Apennine Mountains.

Garisenda, noticeably shorter due to structural instability, leans conspicuously, giving the towers a subtle leaning-tower charm. It's not open to the public, but its dramatic tilt makes it an equally memorable sight, often sparking curiosity about the engineering challenges faced centuries ago.

Beyond their impressive stature, the Two Towers evoke the spirit of a city proud of its history and architectural heritage. Whether you view them from the base, admire them from a café terrace, or climb to the top, these towers are a must-see attraction that connects you directly to Bologna's medieval roots.

Basilica di San Petronio and Other Historic Churches

Bologna's religious architecture offers a window into its spiritual and artistic traditions, with the Basilica di San Petronio standing as a crowning jewel. This vast Gothic church dominates Piazza Maggiore and is one of the largest churches in Europe. Its unfinished façade—part marble, part exposed brick—adds a unique character and hints at the long and complex history behind its construction.

Inside, the basilica impresses with soaring vaults, intricate frescoes, and a richly decorated altar. One of its most fascinating features is the large meridian line on the floor, an astronomical instrument installed in the 17th century that tracks the sun's position—a testament to the blending of science and faith during the Renaissance.

While San Petronio is the star, Bologna is dotted with countless other historic churches worth visiting. Santo Stefano's complex of seven churches offers a labyrinthine journey through different eras and architectural styles. The Church of San Domenico houses works by renowned artists, including Michelangelo, whose sculptural contributions draw art lovers from around the world.

These sacred spaces are not just tourist attractions but living parts of the community. Attending a mass, hearing the choir, or simply sitting in quiet contemplation within these centuries-old walls brings a profound sense of connection to Bologna's cultural soul.

Porticoes: The World's Longest Covered Walkway

Perhaps one of Bologna's most distinctive features—and something that sets it apart from other Italian cities—is its extensive network of porticoes. These elegant covered walkways stretch for over 38 kilometers throughout the city, earning Bologna a spot on UNESCO's World Heritage list. They are not only architecturally stunning but also a practical solution to the city's climate, offering shelter from both the summer sun and winter rain.

Walking under the porticoes feels like traversing a secret world of arches and columns, each one revealing small shops, cafés, and hidden courtyards. The porticoes connect key parts of the city, including the path from the city center to the Sanctuary of the Madonna di San Luca on the hill—a pilgrimage route that locals cherish.

Their history dates back to the Middle Ages when they were built to expand living spaces and provide shelter. Over time, the porticoes evolved into social and commercial arteries, where residents meet, socialize, and conduct daily business. Today, they remain central to Bologna's identity, blending utility with beauty.

Exploring the porticoes offers a unique way to experience the city's rhythm and architecture simultaneously. Whether you're strolling leisurely with a gelato or navigating your way to a specific destination, the porticoes wrap you in Bologna's distinctive ambiance.

Museums and Galleries: Pinacoteca, MAMbo, and More

Bologna's cultural scene extends beyond its streets and churches into a world-class array of museums and galleries that cater to all tastes. From classical art to cutting-edge contemporary exhibitions, the city offers an enriching palette for art lovers and curious travelers alike.

The Pinacoteca Nazionale di Bologna is a treasure trove of Renaissance and Baroque masterpieces. Housing works by artists like Raphael, Titian, and

Guido Reni, it provides a deep dive into Italian art history within an elegant setting. Walking through its halls, you can trace the evolution of styles and themes that shaped European art for centuries.

For those interested in contemporary culture, the Museo d'Arte Moderna di Bologna (MAMbo) offers an engaging collection of modern and contemporary works. It's a dynamic space where exhibitions, performances, and workshops create an immersive cultural experience. MAMbo reflects Bologna's forward-thinking spirit and commitment to nurturing new artistic voices.

Other notable venues include the Archaeological Museum, showcasing Etruscan and Roman artifacts, and the Museum of Music, which celebrates Bologna's rich musical heritage. For a more interactive experience, the Gelato Museum Carpigiani, just outside the city, offers a delicious journey into the history and making of Italy's favorite frozen treat.

Each museum and gallery adds a layer to Bologna's multifaceted identity, providing insight into its past, present, and future. Whether you spend hours exploring grand galleries or pop into a smaller exhibit, these cultural institutions deepen your understanding of the city's creative heart.

Culinary Delights and Food Culture

Bologna's reputation as Italy's culinary capital is no exaggeration. From the moment you step into this city, your senses are greeted by an irresistible aroma of fresh pasta, rich sauces, and baked delights that tell stories of generations devoted to food. It's a place where eating is not just a necessity but an art form, a social ritual, and an essential part of the city's identity. Exploring Bologna's food culture means diving deep into centuries-old traditions, vibrant markets, and lively eateries that serve authentic flavors rooted in the fertile Emilia-Romagna region. This section will take you through the must-try dishes, the best spots to find local produce, immersive food experiences, and the city's unique aperitivo and wine culture, ensuring you savor every bite of your visit.

Traditional Dishes You Can't Miss (Tortellini, Tagliatelle al Ragù)

No trip to Bologna is complete without tasting its legendary pasta dishes, which have become synonymous with Italian gastronomy worldwide. Two classics stand out: tortellini and tagliatelle al ragù. Both embody the rich flavors and painstaking craftsmanship that make Bolognese cuisine so revered.

Tortellini are delicate ring-shaped pasta, traditionally stuffed with a savory mixture of pork loin, prosciutto, and mortadella, combined with Parmesan cheese and eggs. Served in a flavorful capon broth, tortellini is comfort food elevated to a sublime experience. The tiny parcels, each hand-shaped with care, melt in your mouth and transport you to a culinary heritage that has been perfected over centuries. It's no surprise that locals often regard tortellini as a symbol of family, celebration, and tradition.

Tagliatelle al ragù, often mistakenly called spaghetti bolognese abroad, is the true soul food of Bologna. Wide, flat ribbons of fresh egg pasta are generously coated in a slow-cooked ragù—a rich meat sauce made from a blend of beef, pork, tomatoes, onions, carrots, and celery, simmered to perfection. This dish captures the essence of Emilia-Romagna's agricultural bounty and passion for slow, deliberate cooking. Each bite is hearty, fragrant, and deeply satisfying, inviting you to savor the layered flavors that only time can create.

Beyond these staples, Bologna offers other regional specialties like lasagne verdi (lasagna made with spinach pasta sheets), mortadella (a delicately spiced pork sausage), and crescentine (fried bread served with cold cuts and cheeses). Sampling these dishes is essential to understanding why Bologna holds such a cherished place in Italy's culinary landscape.

Best Markets for Local Produce: Quadrilatero & Mercato delle Erbe

To truly appreciate Bologna's food culture, you need to explore its vibrant markets, where tradition and daily life converge in a sensory feast of colors, smells, and flavors. The Quadrilatero area, located near Piazza Maggiore, is an ancient marketplace district bursting with stalls and shops offering the freshest local produce, meats, cheeses, and spices. Walking through the narrow streets of Quadrilatero, you'll encounter vendors enthusiastically displaying seasonal fruits, plump tomatoes, fragrant herbs, and perfectly aged Parmigiano-Reggiano cheese.

The spirit of the market goes beyond shopping—it's a social hub where chefs, locals, and visitors mingle, share recipes, and discuss the day's catch. It's the perfect place to pick up ingredients if you're planning to cook, or just to taste samples of cured meats and freshly baked bread as you wander.

Just a short walk away lies the Mercato delle Erbe, a covered market with a lively atmosphere and a wider range of offerings. Open daily, this market showcases not only produce but also prepared foods, artisanal products, and a variety of dining options. Here, you can find stands selling traditional balsamic vinegar, local wines, truffles, and a wealth of other regional specialties. The market is also home to small eateries where you can grab a quick, authentic meal or sip a cappuccino while watching the hustle and bustle.

Both markets are not only a feast for the palate but also a gateway to understanding the importance of seasonality and locality in Bolognese cuisine. They invite you to connect with the rhythms of the land and the passion of the people who bring these ingredients to life.

Food Tours, Cooking Classes, and Street Food Spots

For those eager to dive deeper into Bologna's gastronomic wonders, food tours and cooking classes offer immersive experiences that go beyond mere tasting. Guided by knowledgeable locals, food tours take you off the beaten path to discover hidden gems, family-run trattorias, and street food stalls serving authentic delights. These tours are a wonderful way to learn the stories behind dishes, meet passionate artisans, and sample a variety of foods in one outing.

Cooking classes provide hands-on opportunities to master classic recipes under the guidance of expert chefs. Whether it's learning to roll fresh pasta or preparing the perfect ragù, these sessions offer a unique blend of education and enjoyment. The shared experience often fosters friendships and leaves lasting memories, along with practical skills to recreate Bologna's flavors at home.

For quick bites and casual dining, Bologna's street food scene is vibrant and varied. From piadine (thin flatbreads filled with cheese, cold cuts, or vegetables) to fried crescentine, street vendors offer tasty, budget-friendly options that capture the city's convivial spirit. Food trucks and stands are especially lively during festivals or weekend markets, adding to the festive ambiance.

Exploring these experiences will enrich your understanding of Bologna's food culture and connect you with the city's warmth and generosity.

Where to Eat Like a Local: Hidden Trattorias and Osterias

While Bologna's popular restaurants and renowned eateries are worth visiting, some of the most memorable meals come from lesser-known trattorias and osterias tucked away in quiet corners of the city. These family-run establishments often operate for generations, serving recipes passed down with pride and care.

Stepping into these intimate spaces, you'll find a warm welcome and menus that highlight seasonal ingredients and traditional cooking methods. The atmosphere is unpretentious yet full of character—wooden tables, chalkboard specials, and the hum of local patrons sharing stories over wine.

Places like Trattoria di Via Serra or Osteria dell'Orsa may not be on every tourist's radar, but they offer authentic dishes prepared with love and expertise. Here, you can savor slow-cooked meats, fresh handmade pasta, and local cheeses paired with regional wines. The chefs often take pride in offering lesser-known specialties and adapting to seasonal changes, ensuring a fresh and genuine dining experience.

Eating in these hidden gems connects you to Bologna's everyday life and culinary heritage in a way that bigger, flashier restaurants sometimes can't match. It's dining with a local's heart, where each meal feels like a celebration.

Aperitivo and Wine Culture in Bologna

As evening falls, Bologna's food culture shifts toward one of Italy's most beloved rituals: the aperitivo. This pre-dinner tradition involves sipping a glass of wine or a spritz while enjoying small plates of snacks and finger foods. It's a social occasion that embodies the Italian art of leisure, conversation, and anticipation of the meal to come.

In Bologna, the aperitivo scene is lively and varied, ranging from chic wine bars to cozy neighborhood locales. You'll find locals gathering to unwind, catch up with friends, or meet new people, all accompanied by the clinking of glasses and the buzz of animated conversation.

Wine plays a starring role in this ritual, and Bologna's location in Emilia-Romagna offers access to some of Italy's finest selections. From robust Sangiovese to sparkling Lambrusco, the region's wines perfectly complement the flavors of the local cuisine. Many bars and enotecas showcase regional vintages, providing an excellent opportunity to taste and learn about the wines that define this part of Italy.

Pair your drink with cicchetti (small snacks), olives, cheeses, or slices of mortadella, and you'll experience the perfect balance of flavors that make aperitivo a cherished moment in Bologna's daily rhythm. This tradition captures the city's convivial spirit and provides a delightful way to transition from day to night.

Festivals, Events, and Cultural Experiences

Bologna's vibrant pulse extends far beyond its rich history and culinary excellence—this city thrives on its festivals, events, and deep-rooted cultural traditions that unfold year-round, turning every visit into a unique celebration of art, music, and community. Walking through Bologna at any time of year, you might stumble upon an impromptu street performance, a colorful parade, or an art installation that adds an unexpected spark to the everyday. This section invites you to immerse yourself in the city's lively cultural calendar, where world-class festivals mingle with age-old local customs, creating a dynamic tapestry of experiences that are as engaging as they are authentic.

Annual Events and Celebrations (Bologna Jazz Festival, Fiera del Libro)

Bologna's calendar is studded with remarkable annual events that attract visitors and locals alike, blending global appeal with unmistakable local flavor. One of the city's crown jewels is the Bologna Jazz Festival, an event that has grown into a highlight of the international jazz scene. Each spring, venues throughout the city—from historic theaters to intimate clubs—come alive with a rich program of concerts featuring legendary artists and emerging talents alike. This festival is not just about music; it's a celebration of creativity and community that fills the air with energy and excitement. The jazz performances are often paired with workshops, discussions, and jam sessions that invite audiences to dive deep into the genre's nuances.

Equally significant is the Fiera del Libro, or Bologna Children's Book Fair, held every spring. Though it primarily focuses on children's literature and publishing, its impact ripples across the cultural sphere. This event transforms the city into a buzzing hub of storytelling, illustration, and creativity, drawing authors, illustrators, publishers, and book lovers from around the world. Walking through the fair, you'll witness the power of narratives to connect generations and cultures, with exhibitions, readings, and interactive workshops making it a celebration of imagination and learning.

Beyond these flagship events, Bologna hosts numerous seasonal fairs, food festivals, and celebrations that highlight everything from local wine and cuisine to historical commemorations. The Feast of San Petronio in October, honoring the city's patron saint, is marked by processions, music, and communal gatherings that showcase Bologna's enduring traditions and community spirit. Attending such events offers a glimpse into the city's soul, where past and present intertwine in joyful harmony.

Music and Theater Highlights

Music and theater are deeply woven into Bologna's cultural fabric, offering an array of experiences that appeal to diverse tastes. The city boasts an impressive network of theaters and concert halls, many housed in stunning historic buildings that themselves tell stories of artistic heritage.

The Teatro Comunale di Bologna is the centerpiece of the city's classical music scene, hosting operas, ballets, and orchestral performances of the highest caliber. Its opulent interiors and impeccable acoustics create an unforgettable setting for experiencing works by composers ranging from Verdi to Puccini. Attending a performance here is a step into a tradition that has nurtured Italy's rich musical legacy.

For contemporary music lovers, Bologna's vibrant club scene and smaller venues showcase everything from indie bands to electronic music, jazz, and world music. Throughout the year, you'll find concerts, DJ nights, and open-air festivals that bring a youthful and energetic vibe to the city's nightlife.

Theater also holds a special place in Bologna's cultural landscape. The city supports a thriving community of playwrights, actors, and experimental artists who push boundaries and explore new forms. Smaller theaters and independent companies offer innovative productions alongside more traditional plays, ensuring that theatergoers can enjoy a broad spectrum of performances. Festivals dedicated to theater and performance art often introduce audiences to international works, creating a rich dialogue between Bologna and the wider cultural world.

Local Traditions and Folklore

Bologna's cultural richness is deeply anchored in its local traditions and folklore, which continue to thrive despite the city's modern pulse. These traditions offer a fascinating window into the collective memory and identity of the Bolognese people, connecting present-day life to centuries of shared stories, customs, and celebrations.

One such tradition is the Palio di Bologna, a historic horse race that traces its origins back to medieval times. Though not as internationally famous as the Palio in Siena, Bologna's version is no less spirited, combining competitive excitement with pageantry and community pride. The event is accompanied by colorful medieval costumes, parades, and music, transporting spectators back to a time when city-states showcased their strength and unity through such competitions.

Folklore also lives on in the city's legends and popular beliefs. Tales of San Petronio, Bologna's patron saint, and various mythical creatures from local lore add an enchanting layer to the city's narrative. These stories often surface in street festivals, public art, and even in the way locals share their history, creating a rich cultural texture that invites visitors to listen and discover.

Religious festivals and celebrations, too, are an integral part of Bologna's tradition. Events marking Easter, Christmas, and other holy days blend solemn rituals with joyous festivities, including communal meals, music, and special markets. These occasions reveal the city's ability to blend spirituality with social connection, creating moments of shared meaning that resonate beyond the religious context.

Art Exhibitions and Temporary Installations

Bologna's artistic spirit is evident not only in its museums and galleries but also through an impressive array of contemporary art exhibitions and temporary installations scattered throughout the city. The city embraces both its historic artistic legacy and the cutting-edge creativity of today's artists, making it a dynamic place for art lovers.

Pinacoteca Nazionale di Bologna offers a stellar collection of Renaissance and Baroque masterpieces, but the city's commitment to contemporary art is equally strong. The Museo d'Arte Moderna di Bologna (MAMbo) is a vibrant hub for modern and contemporary art, frequently hosting exhibitions that challenge, inspire, and provoke thought. These shows feature local, national, and international artists working across diverse media, reflecting current trends and themes in the art world.

Outside traditional gallery walls, Bologna often transforms public spaces with temporary installations that engage residents and visitors alike. These projects can range from large-scale sculptures to immersive multimedia experiences, often designed to spark conversations about urban life, history, or social issues. Walking through the city's streets during such exhibitions is like wandering through an open-air museum where art interacts with everyday life.

Art festivals and biennials also punctuate Bologna's cultural calendar, offering curated programs that celebrate innovation and foster dialogue between artists and the public. These events create a sense of anticipation and excitement, encouraging visitors to explore the city through the lens of contemporary creativity.

Accommodation Options for Every Budget

Whether you're planning a short weekend getaway or a longer immersion in the rhythm of Bologna, finding the right place to stay can significantly shape your experience. Bologna offers a remarkably diverse range of accommodation options, catering to every type of traveler—from the luxury seeker in search of architectural charm to the solo backpacker navigating Europe on a shoestring budget. This city gracefully balances its historical legacy with modern sensibilities, and that balance is clearly reflected in where you can stay.

70

From opulent hotels tucked inside Renaissance palaces to cozy family-run guesthouses on quiet side streets, the variety is not only generous but often uniquely memorable. Let's explore the best options across different budgets and styles of travel, along with smart booking strategies that can make a real difference in comfort and cost.

Boutique Hotels and Luxury Stays

For travelers drawn to elegance, comfort, and thoughtful design, Bologna's boutique and luxury hotels are an experience in themselves. Many are housed in former aristocratic residences or renovated heritage buildings, combining historical architecture with refined contemporary interiors. Staying in such places often feels less like checking into a hotel and more like stepping into a curated slice of Bolognese life.

Boutique hotels in Bologna are rarely flashy. Instead, they tend to emphasize understated luxury, prioritizing locally sourced furnishings, personalized service, and a strong sense of place. Expect charming courtyards, breakfast rooms with vaulted ceilings, and rooms adorned with vintage details. These hotels often have fewer rooms, allowing for a more intimate and tailored experience. Some even include small libraries or wine cellars where you can unwind after a day of exploring.

At the higher end of the spectrum, luxury hotels in Bologna deliver impeccable service alongside indulgent amenities—think rooftop terraces with sweeping views of the medieval skyline, in-house Michelin-starred dining, and spa facilities designed to help you unwind in style. Many are centrally located, making it easy to step outside and immediately find yourself immersed in the historic center. Despite the elegance, these accommodations often retain a warm, inviting atmosphere rather than a sterile formality, staying true to Bologna's character.

Budget-Friendly Hostels and Guesthouses

For travelers keeping a close eye on expenses, Bologna remains a welcoming destination. The city is home to a good number of budget-friendly options that don't skimp on comfort or charm. Hostels in Bologna tend to be clean, safe, and increasingly stylish, often reflecting a design-conscious approach even on a limited budget. Some hostels offer private rooms in addition to traditional dormitories, making them a great option for couples or solo travelers looking for affordable privacy.

Many of these budget accommodations are located just outside the city center—close enough for an easy walk or short bus ride, but far enough to enjoy a quieter night's sleep. What sets Bologna's hostels and guesthouses apart is the sense of community they foster. It's not uncommon to find common rooms filled with books, local artwork, and travelers sharing stories over a glass of Lambrusco. Some offer communal dinners, guided walking tours, or bike rentals, helping guests connect with both the city and each other.

Guesthouses and B&Bs run by local families are another excellent option in the budget-to-midrange category. They often come with thoughtful personal touches—homemade pastries for breakfast, insider recommendations on where to eat, and that unmistakable warmth that turns a temporary stay into something more meaningful.

Apartments and Airbnb Recommendations

For those looking to settle into a neighborhood and experience the city more like a local, renting an apartment or Airbnb can be an ideal choice. Bologna's layout, with its many distinct and walkable districts, makes it easy to find a short-term rental that suits both your itinerary and lifestyle. Whether you're staying for a few nights or a couple of weeks, having your own kitchen and living space adds flexibility and comfort to your stay.

Airbnb listings in Bologna range from minimalist studios to spacious lofts with exposed beams and terracotta floors. Many are located in traditional buildings with character—arched doorways, shuttered windows, and balconies that overlook lively piazzas or quiet courtyards. The best apartments strike a balance between style and practicality, offering strong Wi-Fi, laundry facilities, and fully equipped kitchens alongside tasteful decor.

Renting an apartment is particularly appealing for families, groups, or anyone planning a longer visit. You can shop at local markets, prepare your own meals, and set your own pace for exploring. However, it's worth noting that the popularity of short-term rentals has also made it important to be mindful of local regulations and the impact on housing for residents. Choosing hosts who are licensed and respectful of their neighbors is a simple but important step in being a responsible guest.

Staying in Historic Buildings: Pros and Cons

One of Bologna's greatest charms is its abundance of historic buildings, many of which now house hotels, guesthouses, and rentals. Staying in one of these properties can significantly enhance your visit, wrapping you in centuries-old stories and architectural beauty from the moment you check in. Vaulted ceilings, antique tile floors, frescoed walls, and views of red rooftops or medieval towers create an atmospheric backdrop that few modern hotels can match.

However, not all historic accommodations are created equal, and it's worth considering both the benefits and potential drawbacks. On the plus side, these buildings often have unbeatable locations—nestled in quiet alleys or facing elegant piazzas, close to major landmarks yet insulated from crowds. Their uniqueness can make your stay feel much more personal and immersive.

On the other hand, age can bring limitations. Some buildings may not have elevators, making them less suitable for travelers with mobility issues. Bathrooms might be small, and heating or air conditioning may not be as modern or efficient as in newer properties. Noise insulation can vary depending on the building's structure and location. That said, many historic accommodations have undergone sensitive renovations that address these concerns without sacrificing their charm. If authenticity and atmosphere matter more to you than streamlined amenities, staying in a historic building can be an unforgettable highlight.

Booking Tips for Peak and Off-Peak Seasons

Timing is everything when it comes to booking accommodation in Bologna, especially if you're hoping to balance quality and cost. The city experiences noticeable fluctuations in visitor numbers depending on the season, academic calendar, and major events.

Spring (April to June) and autumn (September to early November) are considered the best times to visit in terms of weather and ambiance. However, they also tend to be the busiest and most expensive, particularly during festivals, trade fairs, and university events. Booking well in advance is strongly recommended for these months, especially if you have your heart set on a particular area or style of accommodation. Prices can rise significantly during these peak times, and last-minute options may be limited.

Summer, though quieter in terms of tourism, can be hot and a bit subdued, as locals head out of town for holidays and some businesses close or reduce their hours. Accommodation rates are often more affordable during this season, and you may find excellent deals on otherwise premium lodgings. Just be sure your accommodation has effective air conditioning.

Winter brings its own charms, especially around the holidays when the city lights up with festive markets and events. While it's colder and darker, it's also less crowded, making it easier to find good deals. This is a great time to enjoy indoor attractions like museums, theaters, and cozy trattorias without the lines or rush.

Regardless of when you plan to visit, flexibility and research go a long way. Use trusted booking platforms, check cancellation policies, and consider booking direct through the accommodation's website when possible—many offer perks or better rates this way. Don't be afraid to reach out to hosts or hotels with questions, especially if you're staying in a smaller or independent place. A bit of communication upfront can ensure your stay goes smoothly and meets your expectations.

Getting Around

Exploring Bologna is a pleasure made even better when you know the ins and outs of getting around efficiently and smoothly. The city's layout, characterized by its medieval charm and expansive porticoes, lends itself wonderfully to walking, while other transportation options offer convenient alternatives for longer distances or when time is tight. Whether you prefer the freedom of a bike, the ease of public transit, or the flexibility of a rental car, understanding how Bologna moves will help you maximize your time and enjoy the city like a local. Let's delve into the best ways to navigate Bologna, along with practical tips that make getting from place to place as enjoyable as the destinations themselves.

Navigating the City on Foot and by Bike

Bologna is, at its heart, a walkable city. The historic center is compact enough to explore comfortably on foot, with charming narrow streets, bustling piazzas, and shaded porticoes inviting leisurely strolls no matter the season. Walking allows you to soak up the atmosphere, spot hidden gems, and wander spontaneously into cafés or artisan shops that catch your eye.

The porticoes—those iconic covered walkways that stretch for nearly 40 kilometers across the city—offer shade from the summer sun and shelter from rain in cooler months. This unique feature makes walking even more pleasant, especially during less predictable weather. The network of pedestrian-friendly alleys and piazzas means you can meander through neighborhoods like the Centro Storico, Santo Stefano, or the University District without needing to rely on any vehicle.

If you enjoy cycling, Bologna is becoming increasingly bike-friendly. Thanks to flat terrain and a growing network of dedicated bike lanes, riding around the city is both practical and enjoyable. You'll find bike rental shops near the train station and throughout the city center, offering everything from classic city bikes to electric models for easier pedaling. Some rental services even provide guided bike tours, combining transport and sightseeing.

Biking is a particularly efficient way to reach areas just beyond the historic center, such as the Bolognina district or the scenic hills surrounding the city. When cycling, it's important to stay aware of traffic and local biking customs, which can differ from what you're used to. Helmets are recommended, and most importantly, be respectful of pedestrians and follow traffic signals.

Public Transit: Buses, Trams, and Tickets

For journeys that extend beyond a comfortable walk or bike ride, Bologna's public transportation network is reliable and straightforward. The city's main transit modes include an extensive bus system and a newer tram line, both operated by TPER (Trasporto Passeggeri Emilia-Romagna).

Together, they connect the historic center with suburbs, train stations, and key points of interest.

Buses in Bologna are frequent and cover a comprehensive set of routes. Many lines intersect at major hubs such as Piazza Maggiore, the Central Train Station (Stazione Centrale), and Fiera District. The tram system, a relatively recent addition to the city's infrastructure, offers a modern, fast, and eco-friendly option on selected corridors, ideal for avoiding traffic jams during rush hours.

Tickets for buses and trams are purchased before boarding and come in various forms: single rides, daily passes, and multi-day cards. You can buy them at newsstands, tobacco shops (tabaccherie), vending machines, or via mobile apps. It's important to validate your ticket once on board by stamping it in the designated machine; failure to do so can result in fines during spot checks. Ticket inspectors are common, especially during peak tourist seasons.

For visitors planning multiple trips in a day or over several days, investing in a daily or multi-day pass is economical and convenient. These passes allow unlimited travel within a set time frame and can simplify spontaneous exploration without the hassle of buying a ticket every time you board.

The public transit system is generally accessible, but some older buses or stops may pose challenges for travelers with reduced mobility. If this is a consideration for you, it's advisable to check routes in advance or seek assistance from transit staff.

Car Rentals and Driving in the ZTL Zone

While Bologna's compact historic center and excellent public transit mean most visitors rarely need a car, renting one can be a smart choice if you plan to explore the surrounding Emilia-Romagna region, countryside, or neighboring cities like Modena, Ferrara, or Florence.

Car rental agencies are plentiful near the train station and airport, offering a wide range of vehicles from economy models to larger vans. Booking in advance often secures the best rates, especially during the busy travel seasons.

That said, driving in Bologna requires some careful planning, particularly because of the city's Zona a Traffico Limitato, or ZTL. This restricted traffic zone covers much of the historic center and is strictly monitored by cameras. Unauthorized vehicles entering the ZTL face substantial fines, which can be issued automatically by mail and may take weeks to arrive. If your accommodation is inside the ZTL, be sure to communicate with your host or hotel—they often provide temporary permits for guests or guidance on where you can legally park.

Parking near the center is limited and often expensive, so if your main goal is to explore central Bologna, relying on walking, biking, or public transit is generally more practical. Many visitors choose to park in designated lots outside the ZTL boundary and then use buses or trams to reach the heart of the city.

For excursions beyond Bologna, driving is a fantastic way to explore rolling hills, vineyards, and charming towns at your own pace. The roads are well-maintained, and highways are clearly marked. Keep in mind that Italian driving habits may differ from what you're accustomed to, so stay alert and patient, especially when navigating roundabouts or narrow village streets.

Day Passes and City Cards: Are They Worth It?

Bologna offers several options for visitors interested in combining transportation with sightseeing perks, and deciding whether a day pass or city card is worthwhile depends largely on your itinerary and preferences.

The Bologna Welcome Card is a popular choice, bundling unlimited public transit rides with entry to a range of museums and attractions, discounts at shops and restaurants, and guided walking tours. If you plan to visit multiple museums and take advantage of public transportation frequently, this card can save you both money and time by skipping lines.

Alternatively, the TPER day or multi-day passes focus solely on transit, providing unlimited bus and tram travel without the extras. These are perfect if your main goal is to explore neighborhoods, attend events, or move between the city center and outskirts without the added need for museum access.

Many visitors appreciate the convenience and flexibility these passes offer, eliminating the need to buy individual tickets and making hopping on and off public transit stress-free. Before purchasing, take a close look at your planned activities and calculate whether the pass matches your usage. For example, if you plan to stay mainly within walking distance of key sights and prefer to take taxis or bikes occasionally, individual tickets might be more economical.

Bologna's transportation system is a blend of historic charm and modern efficiency, perfectly suited to a city that rewards slow, deliberate exploration. Walking remains the best way to absorb the atmosphere, while bikes and public transit expand your reach with ease. Renting a car is best reserved for those who want to venture beyond the city limits, but it comes with its own set of rules to navigate. With a little planning and flexibility, you'll find that getting around Bologna is not just a necessity but a part of the city's unique appeal—inviting you to discover every corner at your own pace.

Day Trips and Surrounding Destinations

Bologna, with its rich history and vibrant urban life, is an exceptional base for exploring some of Italy's most fascinating nearby towns and landscapes. Just a short train ride or drive from the city center, you can dive into diverse experiences ranging from Renaissance art to culinary marvels, and from medieval streets to serene natural escapes. Whether you're a foodie, history enthusiast, or nature lover, the Emilia-Romagna region surrounding Bologna offers rewarding day trips that add depth and variety to your Italian adventure.

Exploring Modena: Balsamic Vinegar and Ferrari Museum

Modena, located about 40 minutes west of Bologna by train, is a compelling destination for those who appreciate both history and gastronomy. The city's heart is a UNESCO World Heritage site, renowned for its beautiful Romanesque cathedral, Torre

Civica, and Piazza Grande. Walking through Modena's streets reveals an elegant blend of medieval and Renaissance architecture, inviting visitors to slow down and savor the atmosphere.

But what truly sets Modena apart is its culinary heritage. This is the birthplace of traditional balsamic vinegar, one of Italy's most treasured culinary exports. Small family-run acetaie (vinegar producers) in the surrounding countryside craft this complex, aged vinegar with remarkable care, often keeping their production methods a closely guarded secret passed down through generations. Visiting a local acetaia offers a rare glimpse into this artisanal process and the chance to taste authentic, aged balsamic vinegar, which is worlds apart from the mass-produced varieties found elsewhere.

Modena is also synonymous with speed and luxury cars, thanks to its ties with Ferrari. The Ferrari Museum, just outside the city, is a must-see for automobile enthusiasts and offers a fascinating insight into the history, engineering, and racing heritage of one of the most iconic brands in the world. Even if you're not a car fanatic, the museum's sleek design and thrilling exhibits, including legendary models and racing memorabilia, make for a captivating visit.

Pair your visit with a meal at one of Modena's acclaimed restaurants—many holding Michelin stars—where chefs elevate traditional Emilian cuisine to fine dining art. The city's culinary reputation, bolstered by native chefs like Massimo Bottura, makes Modena a culinary pilgrimage that beautifully complements its historic charm.

Parma's Culinary and Artistic Treasures

Parma, roughly an hour's journey northwest of Bologna, is another jewel of the Emilia-Romagna region, celebrated for its exquisite food and artistic legacy. Often dubbed the "food capital" of the area, Parma is the home of Parmesan cheese (Parmigiano-Reggiano) and prosciutto di Parma, two staples of Italian cuisine known and loved worldwide.

A day trip here is a chance to immerse yourself in the craftsmanship behind these culinary icons. Many local producers welcome visitors for tours where you can see how Parmesan cheese is carefully aged or how prosciutto undergoes its meticulous curing process. These experiences deepen appreciation for the flavors and textures that make Parma's products so special.

Beyond food, Parma offers a treasure trove of cultural riches. The city's historic center boasts impressive Renaissance architecture, with highlights including the Parma Cathedral, famous for its striking frescoes by Correggio, and the Baptistery, an exquisite example of medieval architecture. The Teatro Regio di Parma is a landmark for opera lovers, hosting world-class performances that celebrate the city's musical heritage.

Strolling through Parma's streets, you'll encounter elegant piazzas, cozy cafés, and inviting trattorias serving up hearty, traditional dishes. The combination of art and cuisine makes Parma a fulfilling destination that appeals to both the mind and the palate.

Ferrara's Renaissance Heritage

Heading northeast from Bologna, Ferrara awaits with its distinctive Renaissance character. About an hour and a half by train, Ferrara offers a different kind of Italian charm—one that centers on the elegant urban planning and cultural flowering of the 15th and 16th centuries under the Este family.

The city's well-preserved Renaissance walls encircle a network of streets and piazzas that feel like stepping into a living museum. The Castello Estense, a moated fortress at the city's center, is a highlight, showcasing lavish interiors and ramparts that provide panoramic views of Ferrara. Wandering along the city walls or cycling on the paths that follow them is a popular way to appreciate Ferrara's blend of history and greenery.

Ferrara's cultural scene includes a thriving calendar of events, such as the annual Ferrara Buskers Festival, celebrating street performers and circus arts, which transforms the city into a vibrant, colorful spectacle each September.

Food lovers will enjoy sampling Ferrara's local specialties, including pumpkin-based dishes and salama da sugo, a traditional spiced pork sausage slow-cooked to perfection. Ferrara's culinary offerings complement the city's artistic ambiance, making it a rewarding day trip destination for those looking to explore beyond the more frequented tourist paths.

Ravenna's Byzantine Mosaics

Further east along the Adriatic coast, Ravenna stands out as one of Italy's greatest artistic treasures. About 90 minutes from Bologna by train, Ravenna is world-famous for its extraordinary collection of early Christian and Byzantine mosaics, some of the best-preserved and most impressive in Europe.

Visiting Ravenna is a journey into the art and spirituality of the 5th and 6th centuries, when it served as the capital of the Western Roman Empire and later the Byzantine Exarchate. The city's UNESCO-listed monuments, such as the Basilica of San Vitale and the Mausoleum of Galla Placidia, offer dazzling mosaics that depict biblical scenes, saints, and intricate geometric patterns in vivid colors that seem to glow even after more than a millennium.

Ravenna's charm extends beyond its mosaics. The city features a relaxed atmosphere, with charming piazzas, lively cafés, and a coastline just a short distance away where visitors can enjoy the Adriatic breeze. A visit here blends art, history, and the gentle pace of a smaller city, making it an enriching complement to your time in Bologna.

Nature Escapes: Apennine Mountains and Wine Regions

For those seeking natural beauty and outdoor adventures, the Emilia-Romagna region offers inviting escapes not far from Bologna. The nearby Apennine Mountains provide lush landscapes, hiking trails, and picturesque villages where you can experience a quieter side of Italian life.

Just a short drive or bus ride from Bologna, the Apennines are ideal for hiking in spring and summer, with routes ranging from easy walks to challenging climbs. In winter, some areas turn into charming ski resorts, offering a welcome change of scenery and a chance to enjoy snow sports. The fresh mountain air, combined with stunning views of rolling hills and forests, makes this a refreshing getaway from city bustle.

Wine lovers will appreciate the proximity of several renowned wine-producing areas, including the Colli Bolognesi and Lambrusco regions. Visiting vineyards and wineries here offers an immersive experience in Italian viticulture, complete with tastings of robust reds, sparkling whites, and the region's famous Lambrusco sparkling red wine.

Many wineries open their doors for tours and intimate tastings, often paired with local cheeses and cured meats. Exploring these rural landscapes by car or bike lets you connect with the region's agricultural heritage and savor authentic flavors in a beautiful, pastoral setting.

Shopping, Markets, and Artisan Crafts

Bologna's vibrant culture is beautifully reflected in its bustling shopping scene, where historic markets, artisan workshops, and chic boutiques come together to create a rich tapestry of retail experiences. For visitors eager to take a piece of the city home, whether that's a handcrafted souvenir, a fashion statement, or fresh local produce, Bologna offers an authentic blend of tradition and modern style. Exploring its shops and markets reveals the city's dedication to craftsmanship, quality, and creativity, all woven into daily life.

Where to Find Local Handicrafts and Souvenirs

If you're looking for souvenirs that capture the essence of Bologna, the city's artisan shops are the perfect places to discover unique, handcrafted items. Walking through the narrow streets near the historic center, you'll find ateliers and workshops where skilled artisans create everything from ceramics to leather goods, textiles to delicate jewelry.

One of the hallmarks of Bologna's craft scene is the dedication to traditional techniques passed down through generations. Handmade ceramics often feature classic Italian designs, with subtle nods to the city's medieval and Renaissance heritage. Leather artisans craft wallets, belts, and bags using supple hides, combining durability with elegance. Visiting these shops is more than just shopping — it's an opportunity to witness the passion and skill behind each creation.

For those who appreciate fine stationery and bookbinding, Bologna's history as a university city has fostered a flourishing culture of paper arts. Small shops sell beautifully crafted notebooks, journals, and calligraphy supplies, perfect gifts for travelers who cherish writing or sketching.

If you want a true taste of local flavor in souvenir form, look for specialty food items such as bottles of traditional balsamic vinegar, jars of honey from the Apennine hills, or artisanal pastas shaped by hand. These edible treasures not only taste incredible but also tell stories of the region's culinary legacy.

Shopping for Italian Fashion and Design

Beyond crafts, Bologna's shopping scene is a vibrant mix of Italian fashion and design, blending both international labels and local brands. Though not as globally famous as Milan or Florence, Bologna's boutiques offer a refined selection of apparel and accessories that reflect Italy's renowned style—timeless, elegant, and crafted with attention to detail.

In the central shopping streets such as Via Rizzoli and Via Indipendenza, you'll find flagship stores for major Italian brands alongside smaller, independent boutiques showcasing emerging designers. These shops often feature clothing and accessories that emphasize quality fabrics, craftsmanship, and understated luxury, catering to shoppers who prefer classic, versatile pieces over fleeting trends.

Via Rizzoli

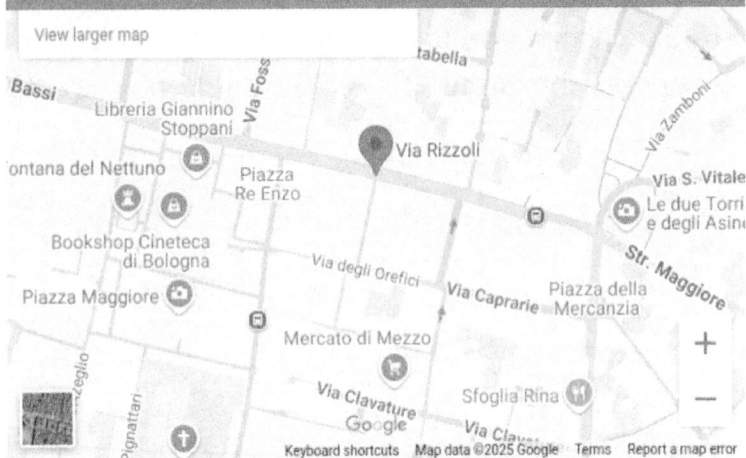

SCAN THE QR CODE

- Open your phone's camera app
- Most smartphones have a built-in QR scanner in the camera.
- Point the camera at the QR code
- Make sure the code is clear and within the frame.
- Wait for the notification
- A link or message should pop up on your screen
- Tap the notification
- This will open the link or content in your browser or a relevant app.
- Follow the instructions on the screen
- You will be taken to a Google Maps, app where you can now click on your current location to get to your destination.

One of the pleasures of shopping in Bologna is discovering local designers who infuse their work with a sense of place. From handcrafted shoes to bespoke tailoring, these labels offer pieces that can't be found elsewhere, making your purchases both stylish and uniquely Bolognese.

In addition to fashion, the city is known for its excellent home design stores and artisan studios specializing in ceramics, glassware, and furniture. Whether you're looking for a modern lamp or a hand-painted vase, these shops reflect Italy's commitment to marrying form with function.

Markets for Fresh Food and Specialty Products

No discussion of shopping in Bologna would be complete without visiting its legendary markets, where fresh food, specialty products, and lively social interactions define the experience. The city's markets are more than just places to buy groceries — they are community hubs where locals gather, share stories, and celebrate the region's abundant culinary traditions.

The Quadrilatero district, just off Piazza Maggiore, is the historic market heart of Bologna. Here, narrow streets are lined with stalls and small shops selling everything from freshly baked bread and aged cheeses to fragrant spices and succulent meats. The vibrant colors and rich aromas create a sensory feast that invites exploration. Sampling cured meats such as mortadella, a Bologna specialty, is a must.

Another important market is the Mercato delle Erbe, a lively indoor market offering a wide range of fresh produce, meats, fish, and dairy products. It's a favorite spot among locals for everyday shopping and for finding seasonal specialties. Wandering through the Mercato delle Erbe, you can strike up conversations with vendors who are often eager to share recipes and tips, adding an invaluable layer of local knowledge to your visit.

Specialty shops around these markets offer regional delicacies such as Parmigiano-Reggiano cheese, prosciutto di Parma, and various types of fresh pasta. These ingredients, known worldwide but best experienced here, make excellent gifts and personal souvenirs.

Tips for Bargaining and Ethical Shopping

When shopping in Bologna's markets and artisan shops, a few guidelines can help you have a rewarding and respectful experience. While Italy is generally not a culture of aggressive haggling, polite bargaining can sometimes be appropriate, especially in open-air markets or smaller family-run stalls. Engaging with vendors with a friendly attitude and genuine interest can sometimes result in small discounts or extra items.

For fixed-price boutiques, particularly those selling high-end fashion or handcrafted goods, prices tend to be firm, reflecting the quality and effort invested in the products. However, asking about upcoming sales or promotions is always acceptable, especially if you're planning to make multiple purchases.

Ethical shopping is increasingly important, and Bologna offers many opportunities to support sustainable and responsible businesses. Look for shops that emphasize locally sourced materials, eco-friendly production methods, and fair labor practices. Many artisan workshops proudly share their commitment to these values, which helps preserve traditional crafts while protecting the environment.

Markets also offer a chance to support local farmers and producers, contributing directly to the community. Choosing seasonal fruits and vegetables not only guarantees freshness but also reduces the carbon footprint associated with long-distance transportation.

Practical Tips for a Smooth Visit

Traveling to Bologna, like any journey to a foreign city, comes with its own set of practical considerations that can help ensure your trip is enjoyable, safe, and hassle-free. From mastering a few key phrases in Italian to understanding local health services, staying connected, managing money matters, and embracing sustainable tourism, these practical tips will empower you to make the most of your time in this vibrant city. Whether you're a first-time visitor or returning for another adventure, having these essentials at your fingertips will smooth your path and deepen your connection to Bologna's culture.

Language Basics and Useful Phrases

While many people in Bologna's tourism and service industries speak English, dipping into a few Italian phrases will not only help you navigate daily interactions but also earn you warm smiles and appreciation from locals. Italian is a melodic and expressive language, and even a small effort to use it demonstrates respect and interest in the culture.

Start with simple greetings such as "Buongiorno" (Good morning) or "Buonasera" (Good evening). When entering shops, cafes, or restaurants, a friendly "Salve" or "Ciao" (informal hello) sets a positive tone. Knowing how to say "Per favore" (please) and "Grazie" (thank you) goes a long way. If you need assistance, phrases like "Parla inglese?" (Do you speak English?) or "Mi può aiutare?" (Can you help me?) are handy.

For ordering food or asking for directions, familiarize yourself with key vocabulary: "Il conto, per favore" (The bill, please), "Dove si trova...?" (Where is...?), and "Quanto costa?" (How much does it cost?). Don't worry about perfect pronunciation — Italians tend to appreciate the effort regardless.

Carrying a small phrasebook or a translation app on your phone is wise. It can assist you in more specific situations such as medical emergencies or transport queries. Many useful apps offer offline capabilities, which is helpful in areas with limited internet.

Health and Safety: Emergency Numbers and Pharmacies

Knowing how to respond to health or safety concerns is essential for any traveler. Bologna is generally safe, with excellent healthcare facilities and attentive emergency services, but being prepared is always prudent.

In case of emergency, the general European emergency number 112 works throughout Italy and connects you to police, fire, and medical assistance. For a direct medical emergency, dialing 118 will get you in touch with ambulance services. It's a good idea to have these numbers saved in your phone and written down in case of phone issues.

Pharmacies, or "farmacie," are widely available across the city. They not only dispense medications but also provide advice on minor ailments and first aid. Many pharmacies operate regular hours during the week, and several rotate on duty during nights and weekends, known as "farmacia di turno." Look for a green cross sign that glows outside the pharmacy.

If you have ongoing medical conditions or take prescription medications, bring a sufficient supply with you and copies of your prescriptions. While many medicines are available in Bologna, some brands or formulations might differ. Travel insurance with medical coverage is highly recommended and can ease the process if you require professional care.

Safety-wise, Bologna is considered a secure city, but like many tourist destinations, pickpocketing can occur, especially in crowded areas or on public transportation. Keeping your belongings close and being aware of your surroundings will help you avoid common scams or theft.

Connectivity: SIM Cards, Wi-Fi Spots, and Apps

Staying connected during your trip can greatly enhance your experience, whether it's for navigation, translation, booking tickets, or simply sharing moments with friends and family. Bologna offers good options for mobile and internet access, accommodating both short-term visitors and longer stays.

Many international travelers find it convenient to purchase a local prepaid SIM card upon arrival. Major Italian mobile providers like TIM, Vodafone, and WindTre have shops at Bologna's airport and around the city center. Prepaid plans offer various data packages at affordable prices and can be topped up easily online or in stores. Remember to check your phone's compatibility with local networks and bring your passport for SIM registration.

Wi-Fi is widely available in hotels, cafes, restaurants, museums, and public squares. However, signal quality may vary, so having mobile data ensures uninterrupted access. When using public Wi-Fi, exercise caution by avoiding sensitive transactions unless you're on a secure network or using a VPN.

Several smartphone apps are invaluable for navigating Bologna. The TPER app helps with public transport schedules and ticket purchases. Google Maps and Citymapper provide walking and transit directions. For dining, apps like The Fork or Yelp offer reviews and reservations. Language apps and offline translators can bridge any communication gaps.

Before traveling, download any necessary apps and store offline maps or guides for convenience, especially if you anticipate limited internet access during excursions.

Money Matters: ATMs, Credit Cards, and Tipping Customs

Handling money in Bologna is straightforward but knowing local customs and practical tips will help you avoid surprises and manage your budget effectively.

ATMs ("bancomat") are plentiful throughout the city, including at the airport, train stations, and near tourist attractions. Most international debit and credit cards are accepted, but it's wise to notify your bank in advance of your travel to prevent card blocks. Keep an eye on withdrawal fees and exchange rates, which vary depending on your bank.

Cash remains king for many small purchases, markets, and some family-run shops or trattorias. Having a modest amount of euros in coins and notes is practical for tips, bus tickets, or quick snacks.

Credit and debit cards are widely accepted in hotels, restaurants, and larger stores. Visa and Mastercard are the most commonly used, while American Express may not be as universally accepted. Contactless payments have become increasingly popular, so your smartphone or card's contactless feature can be very convenient.

Tipping in Bologna is appreciated but not obligatory. A service charge ("coperto") is usually included in restaurant bills, covering bread and table settings. If service is excellent, leaving a 5–10% tip is generous. For cafes or bars, rounding up the bill or leaving small change is customary. Taxi drivers, hotel porters, and guides generally appreciate small tips as a thank-you for good service.

Currency exchange counters are available but often offer less favorable rates than ATMs or banks. It's advisable to exchange only small amounts at counters or upon arrival and use ATMs for withdrawals.

Sustainable and Responsible Tourism Practices

Bologna is increasingly mindful of its environmental impact and encourages visitors to engage in responsible tourism that respects local culture, preserves heritage, and supports the community.

One of the easiest ways to contribute is by using sustainable transport options. Walking and biking are excellent ways to explore Bologna's compact historic center while reducing carbon emissions. Public transportation, including buses and trams, offers eco-friendly alternatives to cars.

When shopping or dining, prioritize locally sourced and seasonal products. This supports regional farmers and artisans and reduces the environmental footprint associated with imported goods. Choosing restaurants that emphasize organic or traditional cooking methods is another way to enjoy Bologna's food culture responsibly.

Respecting local customs and traditions goes hand-in-hand with sustainability. Dress modestly when visiting churches and historic sites, and follow guidelines on photography or access to sensitive areas. Engaging with locals respectfully and learning about their culture enriches your experience and fosters mutual understanding.

Waste reduction is a growing focus. Carrying a reusable water bottle and shopping bags helps minimize plastic use. Many public drinking fountains ("nasoni") provide fresh, safe water, making it easy to refill throughout the day. Dispose of litter thoughtfully and use recycling bins where available.

Supporting small businesses over large chains benefits the local economy and preserves the city's unique character. When booking tours or experiences, opt for certified guides or companies with sustainable practices.

113

Conclusion and Insider Advice

As your journey through Bologna draws to a close, it's worth taking a moment to reflect on what makes this city truly special and how you can continue to experience it—and the wider Emilia-Romagna region—in a way that goes beyond the typical tourist itinerary. Bologna isn't just a destination; it's a living, breathing mosaic of history, culture, food, and community. To experience it like a local means embracing its rhythm, appreciating its nuances, and uncovering the hidden layers that many visitors miss.

Final Thoughts on Experiencing Bologna Like a Local

Bologna's charm lies in its ability to balance tradition and modernity, history and innovation, vibrant student life, and age-old craftsmanship. To see beyond the postcard views of the Two Towers or the elegant arcades, take the time to slow down and live the city from a local's perspective. Early mornings at the neighborhood cafés where shopkeepers greet each other by name, afternoons spent wandering through artisan workshops, and evenings lingering in a quiet piazza with a glass of Lambrusco are moments that reveal the soul of the city.

One of the best ways to feel at home here is to explore the lesser-known neighborhoods. The Santo Stefano district, with its labyrinth of medieval churches and tranquil streets, offers a peaceful retreat from the bustling city center. Meanwhile, the university district pulses with youthful energy, street art, and bohemian cafés—perfect for soaking in Bologna's contemporary creative scene.

Don't hesitate to strike up conversations with locals. Bolognesi take pride in their city and its culinary heritage, and many enjoy sharing stories or recommending their favorite trattorias, bookshops, or scenic walks. The warmth of these exchanges can transform a simple visit into a meaningful connection.

Above all, keep your curiosity alive. Attend a local jazz concert, join a food market tour, or participate in one of the many cultural festivals that animate Bologna's calendar. These experiences deepen your understanding and appreciation, turning you from a visitor into a temporary citizen.

How to Keep Exploring Emilia-Romagna Beyond Bologna

While Bologna is a captivating hub, Emilia-Romagna itself is a region bursting with treasures waiting to be discovered. Just beyond the city's borders lie landscapes and towns that embody Italy's rich cultural tapestry, from culinary excellence to Renaissance art and breathtaking nature.

A short train ride west will take you to Modena, a city synonymous with balsamic vinegar and Ferrari heritage. Here, you can tour traditional vinegar cellars, witnessing the patient craftsmanship that transforms grape must into liquid gold, or visit the Ferrari Museum to immerse yourself in the history of Italian automotive design and innovation.

Parma beckons with its sumptuous food traditions—think Parmigiano-Reggiano cheese and prosciutto di Parma—and its artistic gems, including the breathtaking frescoes in the Farnese Theatre and the elegant architecture that lines its streets. This city invites food lovers and art aficionados alike to indulge their passions.

Eastward lies Ferrara, a Renaissance jewel characterized by its well-preserved city walls, stately palaces, and quiet canals. It's a place to wander slowly, savoring the atmosphere of a city that once flourished as a cultural and intellectual center.

Further to the southeast, Ravenna is renowned for its spectacular Byzantine mosaics—brilliant, shimmering artworks that transform churches into treasures of early Christian art. Exploring Ravenna's UNESCO World Heritage sites offers a glimpse into an ancient world that still pulses with vibrant color.

For nature lovers, the Apennine Mountains provide refreshing escapes with hiking trails, charming villages, and opportunities to experience rural

Emilia-Romagna life. The region's wine areas, including the Colli Bolognesi hills, offer scenic vineyards and welcoming wineries where you can taste some of Italy's finest reds and whites.

Exploring these destinations can be done as day trips or extended stays, each enriching your understanding of the cultural and natural wealth that defines this remarkable region.

Recommended Reading and Resources

To further immerse yourself in the essence of Bologna and Emilia-Romagna, a wealth of books and online resources are available that blend travel insights with history, culture, and gastronomy.

Classic guidebooks provide practical information, but for a deeper dive, consider memoirs and narratives by local writers who capture the city's character with nuance and affection. Books on Italian culinary traditions, particularly those focusing on pasta-making and regional cheeses, offer mouthwatering context to the meals you'll savor.

Magazines and websites dedicated to Italian culture and travel frequently feature Bologna's events, restaurant openings, and new cultural venues, keeping you updated on the city's evolving scene. Following local blogs or social media accounts run by Bolognese artists, chefs, or historians can provide insider perspectives and timely tips.

When it comes to practical planning, official tourism websites offer invaluable information on transport, accommodation, and event calendars. Many include downloadable maps and apps that can enhance your visit.

Equipping yourself with these resources before and during your stay enables a richer, more informed exploration and often leads to unexpected discoveries.

Contact Info for Tourist Offices and Support

Should you need assistance during your trip, Bologna's tourist offices provide friendly, knowledgeable support in multiple languages. The main tourist information center, located near

Piazza Maggiore, is a great starting point for maps, tickets, and recommendations.

Additionally, many neighborhoods have smaller offices or kiosks where staff can answer questions and help with bookings. These centers also offer brochures on local events, museums, and guided tours.

For those traveling with specific needs or interests—whether accessibility accommodations or specialized cultural programs—staff can guide you toward tailored options. It's worth noting that many services now provide online chat support or social media contact points, making it easy to get help even before arrival.

Keeping the contact details of these offices handy ensures peace of mind, allowing you to focus on enjoying your experience without worry.

Bonus: Secret Spots and Off-the-Beaten-Path Ideas

While Bologna's major landmarks are undoubtedly captivating, some of the city's true magic lies in its hidden corners and less-touristed spots. Discovering these places is like stepping into a secret world where time seems to slow, and the city's authenticity shines through.

For example, tucked away near the University district is the Orto Botanico, a serene botanical garden that offers a peaceful respite from urban bustle. Its collection of plants and quiet paths invites moments of reflection and nature appreciation.

The Biblioteca Salaborsa, more than just a library, features an archaeological site visible through glass floors, blending history with modern knowledge. Spending time here connects you with layers of Bologna's past right in the heart of the city.

Venture into the Quadrilatero market area early in the morning to witness locals buying fresh produce, meats, and cheeses, absorbing the vibrant colors and aromas before the crowds arrive. Nearby, small artisan shops craft everything from handmade pasta to traditional ceramics.

If you enjoy panoramic views, climb the less-frequented San Michele in Bosco hill, where you'll be rewarded with sweeping vistas of the red rooftops and surrounding countryside.

For an unusual cultural experience, seek out one of Bologna's many music venues that showcase emerging local talent, or attend a theater performance in smaller, intimate settings rather than the large theaters.

Lastly, taking a bike ride along the city's quieter lanes or exploring the surrounding countryside by foot can reveal charming farmsteads, medieval castles, and small villages untouched by mass tourism.

These hidden gems invite you to explore Bologna's soul beyond guidebooks and postcards, making your visit uniquely memorable.

Printed in Dunstable, United Kingdom